THE SIOUX

ELAINE LANDAU

THE SIOUX

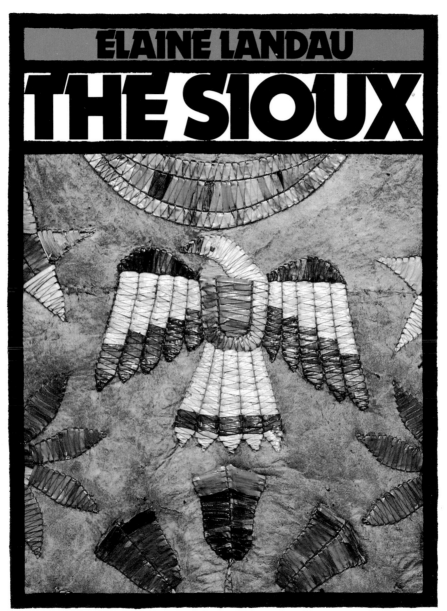

Franklin Watts   New York   London   Toronto   Sydney   A First Book   1989

Map by Joe LeMonnier
Cover photograph courtesy of Museum of the American Indian

Photographs courtesy of: American Museum of Natural History: pp.
10, 14 (bottom), 18, 26 (top), 31; Smithsonian Institution: p. 14 (top);
Amon Carter Museum of Western Art: pp. 15, 35; Gilcrease Institute:
pp. 19, 22, 34; Peabody Museum: pp. 21, 32; Bettmann Archive: p. 25
(top); Buffalo Bill Historical Center, Cody, Wyoming: p. 25 (bottom);
Museum of the American Indian: p. 26 (bottom); Richard Erdoes: p.
29; Coffrins Old West Gallery, Miles City, Montana: p. 30; Granger
Collection: pp. 39, 43, 48, 51, 52; National Archives, Bureau of Indian
Affairs: p. 47; Photo Researchers: pp. 3 (Tom McHugh), 55 (Paolo
Koch), 57 (Farrell Grehan); The Stock Market: p. 56.

Library of Congress Cataloging-in-Publication Data

Landau, Elaine.
The Sioux / by Elaine Landau.
p.   cm.
Bibliography: p.
Includes index.
Summary: Describes the history, customs, religion, and day-to-day
life of the Sioux (also known as Dakota) Indians of the Great Plains.
ISBN 0-531-10754-X
1. Dakota Indians—Juvenile literature.   2. Indians of North
America—Great Plains—Juvenile literature. [1. Dakota Indians.
2. Indians of North America.]   I. Title.
E99.D1L25   1989
978'.00497—dc19   89-5654   CIP   AC

CONTENTS

For Karen Breen
and Ellen Libretto

THE SIOUX

BUFFALO HIDE TIPIS WERE COMFORTABLE DWELLINGS.
DURING THE WINTER MONTHS, A FIRE WAS KEPT
BLAZING IN THE FLOOR'S CENTER TO PROVIDE BOTH
WARMTH AND HEAT FOR COOKING. IN HOT WEATHER,
THE LOWER PORTION OF THE COVERING WAS ROLLED UP
TO ALLOW THE COOL AIR TO ENTER AND CIRCULATE.

THE SIOUX— INDIANS OF THE PLAINS

It was nightfall at the camp. The air was silent except for the sound of the wind and the occasional whine of the horses. The tipis shone brightly from the fire that burned within. By dawn the area would be bustling with activity. Bluish white smoke would rise from the cooking fires. Families would gather for the morning meal. The tipis and the sites on which they stood provided shelter and protection for a very proud and brave people. These were the portable homes of the Sioux Indians.

Long before Columbus came to America, the Sioux traveled from the East Coast of the United States to the western Great Lakes. There, in villages scattered throughout the woodlands of Minnesota, they lived by farming and gathering wild rice. The Sioux also hunted woodland animals and fished.

They traveled by birchbark canoe and used snowshoes in the winter. Some Sioux made seasonal trips each year to hunt the buffalo on the edge of the plains. However, very few Sioux crossed the Mississippi during this time, and none lived west of the Mississippi.

Toward the end of the seventeenth century, some Sioux bands moved westward, across the Mississippi, to the prairie lands adjacent to the plains. On the prairie lands, north and east of the Missouri River, they trapped animals and fished. At times they traded pelts with white traders for European goods.

The Sioux nation was composed of seven groups known as the Seven Council Fires. Each Council Fire had a separate leadership as well as its own band of people who traveled and camped together.

A Sioux camp, which might consist of hundreds of people, could pack up and move on short notice. Before they had horses, the Sioux traveled on foot. They used dogs to pull their belongings and supplies. Their bundles were carried on a device called a *travois*. A travois consisted of two long poles—one end of each pole was fastened to the dog's shoulders, while the other ends trailed behind on the ground. Between the poles baggage was tied to a netlike frame.

Life for the Sioux Indians greatly changed in the eighteenth century after they got horses. The Sioux were excellent riders and horse breeders. Now they

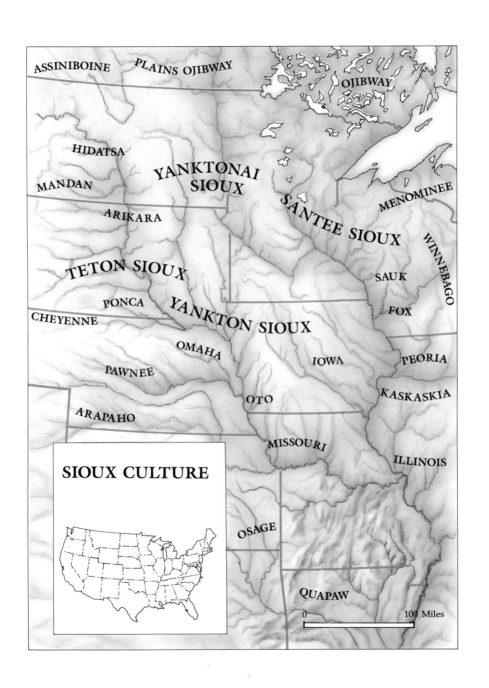

ASSINIBOINE PLAINS OJIBWAY OJIBWAY

HIDATSA

YANKTONAI SIOUX MENOMINEE

MANDAN SANTEE SIOUX

ARIKARA WINNEBAGO

TETON SIOUX SAUK

PONCA FOX

CHEYENNE YANKTON SIOUX

OMAHA IOWA PEORIA

PAWNEE KASKASKIA

OTO

ARAPAHO

MISSOURI ILLINOIS

SIOUX CULTURE

OSAGE

QUAPAW

0   100 Miles

TOP: AS THE SIOUX TRAVELED, THE WOMEN
OVERSAW THE TRAVOISES. DOGS THAT PULLED
SUPPLIES WERE OFTEN UNRULY AND NEEDED
TO BE SEPARATED. KEEPING ORDER AMONG
THE ANIMALS COULD BE A DIFFICULT TASK.
BOTTOM: THE SIOUX TRAVELED TOGETHER IN
GROUPS. AT THE REAR WERE MEN WHO CARRIED
ONLY WEAPONS AS THEY GUARDED THE OTHERS.

THE HORSE HELPED THE INDIANS TO COVER
MUCH FARTHER DISTANCES IN THEIR SEARCH
FOR THE BUFFALO. SCOUTS WENT AHEAD OF
THE BAND TO LOOK OUT FOR ENEMIES.

lived by hunting the bountiful plains buffalo herds. Skilled Sioux rode rapidly with the wind, while darting among the herds of buffalo. As the buffalo roamed, the Sioux followed.

The plains people viewed the horse with a sense of admiration and respect. It could pull or carry four times as much as a dog. A horse could also travel twice the distance in a single day. Since it now replaced the dog as a carrier in their travels, the Sioux called the horse Spirit Dog, Holy Dog, or Medicine Dog.

The horse's value to the Indians who lived on the plains cannot be overestimated. In battle as well as on buffalo hunts, the animal's swiftness, endurance, and obedience might mean the difference between life and death for its owner.

THE BUFFALO

The Sioux Indians depended on the buffalo for survival. They used the animal to meet their most basic needs. But capturing buffalo involved a good deal of danger and difficulty.

Once a group of buffalo had been sighted, the hunters set off on a gallop across the rugged terrain. They would try to herd the buffalo into a circle to make the animals easier prey. The horse was keenly aware of its owner's purpose in the hunt and could be guided by the rider's knee pressure alone. The horses quickly darted in and out of the herds. This allowed the riders to get a better shot at their mark.

The end of a successful hunt was a time for celebration at the camp. Those who had stayed behind cheered the returning hunters. In preparation for a feast, the meat racks stood ready while the cooking fires

EVEN AFTER THE PLAINS INDIANS ACQUIRED GUNS, ONLY BOWS
AND ARROWS OR SPEARS WERE USED IN THE BUFFALO HUNT.
RIFLES WERE TOO HEAVY TO CARRY AND TOO SLOW TO RELOAD.

THE BUFFALO DANCE WAS AN IMPORTANT SIOUX
RITUAL. MOST OF WHAT THE INDIANS NEEDED TO
LIVE COULD BE TAKEN FROM THE BUFFALO.

blazed. Later that night everyone would dance in celebration to the beat of a drum. Now their survival was certain.

The Indians used nearly every part of the buffalo. Sioux infants were wrapped in the soft skin of young buffalo calves. Buffalo hides were also used as shrouds for the dead in burial ceremonies. Parts of the hides and pelts were fashioned into drums, rattles, and battle shields.

The Indians were skilled at tanning buffalo hides to soften them. This helped them to make durable moccasins, leggings, shirts, gloves, jackets, vests, and dresses for themselves. Thicker buffalo skins served as blankets and were also made into heavier robes for the cold winter months. Buffalo rawhide proved to be especially useful in making tools and weapons.

Buffalo meat was the Sioux's major food source. Following a hunt, the tribe enjoyed the meat roasted as well as raw. What was left of it was cured and dried on the racks. It was later cut into edible strips called jerky.

Buffalo meat was also pounded together with fat and wild berries to form a substance called *pemmican*. Pemmican was a nutritious high-protein food. Like buffalo jerky, it could easily be carried and eaten on the trail.

THE SIOUX MADE MANY OBJECTS
FROM BUFFALO HIDE, SUCH AS AN
ARROW CASE (TOP), MOCCASIN (LEFT),
AND A MEDICINE SHIELD (RIGHT).

OFTEN THE SIOUX PAINTED THEIR TIPI
COVERINGS WITH SCENES FROM THEIR DAILY LIFE.
PLANTS, ANIMALS, AND OTHER ASPECTS OF NATURE
WERE COMMON IN THEIR ARTWORK.

The hides of the buffalo were sewn together by Sioux women as coverings for the tipis. A tipi contained most of what its inhabitants needed for daily life. It would be stocked with a supply of food, fuel, medicine, and other household items.

The tipi was an ideal home for the Sioux. It was sturdy enough to withstand the harsh winds of the Great Plains, yet light enough to be taken apart in minutes. And a tipi could be easily transported on a travois when the Sioux traveled.

GAMES, MUSIC, AND ART

Games were a part of everyday life for the Sioux. Often the children's games had a special purpose. Many sporting events helped young boys develop important skills they would need later in life.

Small boys used little bows to practice archery. They began to learn hunting skills at an early age. It was also considered important for Sioux Indians to be swift and able runners. In order to develop speed and endurance, children took part in various running games and contests. During the winter, many Sioux children were given sleds made out of scrapped buffalo bones and pieces of wood.

Adults had their own games. In a popular hand game, someone would try to conceal a small trinket in the palm of his or her hand. The other players had to guess which hand held the object. Sometimes this game would last all night.

LACROSSE PLAYING
AMONG THE SIOUX.
SPORTS AND
GAMES WERE AN
IMPORTANT PART
OF TRIBAL LIFE.

YOUNG
SIOUX GIRLS
WERE USUALLY
GIVEN DOLLS
AND TOY TIPIS
TO PLAY WITH.
AT TIMES,
HOWEVER, THEY
WERE INVITED
TO TAKE PART
IN PHYSICALLY
ACTIVE SPORTS.

COURTING IN A BLANKET WAS AN INNOCENT CUSTOM THAT TOOK PLACE IN FRONT OF THE GIRL'S FAMILY'S TIPI. THE BOY AND GIRL WOULD STAND WITH A BLANKET WRAPPED AROUND THEM AND WHISPER THEIR FEELINGS TO ONE ANOTHER.

SOME HEAVILY BEADED MOCCASINS HAD SEPARATE LEATHER SOLES. WORN ONLY ON AN EXTREMELY FORMAL OCCASION, THEY WERE USUALLY OWNED BY WEALTHY TRIBE MEMBERS.

Games, as well as many of the other activities of the Sioux, were often accompanied by music and songs. There were ceremonial songs for special occasions, war or battle songs, lullabies for babies, and funeral songs.

Music also played an important role in courting and romance. A young man played his flute to let a special girl know his feelings for her. During a quiet night on the plains, the sound of a flute carried a considerable distance.

Art was an important part of Sioux life also. Sioux paintings were of several types. Some paintings were the result of a vision. These pictures were thought to have supernatural powers.

The Sioux also used art to record important events. At times paintings or designs told of the artist's bravery in battle or during the hunt. The Sioux also painted buffalo robes, various types of containers, and tipi coverings. The colors used by the artists had special meanings. To the Sioux, black was the color for night, while red was used to portray thunder and sunsets.

In addition to their paintings, the Sioux did spectacular beadwork in a rich variety of colors. Sioux women sewed brightly colored strings of beads onto buffalo hide to decorate war shirts, moccasins, leggings, and other articles of clothing. Heavily beaded clothing was used as ceremonial garments and worn on special occasions.

RELIGION

Sioux religious beliefs were intense and extremely personal. The Sioux god was Wakan Tanka, also called the Grandfather Spirit or the Great Mystery Power. The Sioux believed that the Great Mystery Power had no beginning or end but instead was in all of nature.

Sioux boys were considered men after going on a vision quest. Experiencing a vision meant having a direct encounter with the Great Mystery Power. Wakan Tanka might appear to the boy in the form of an animal or even an insect.

Before beginning a vision quest, the boy purified himself by sweating in a lodge especially built for this purpose. Then the boy would climb to a deserted hilltop. There he would remain crouched in a vision pit for as long as three to four days. During this period he would have no food and wear only a breechcloth and moccasins. It was a difficult and lonely task.

ON A VISION QUEST, A YOUNG BOY HAD TO
STRUGGLE TO SEE BENEATH THE SURFACE OF
WHAT APPEARED TO BE REAL. IF HIS QUEST
WERE SUCCESSFUL, THE VISION WOULD HELP
TO DETERMINE HIS FUTURE TRIBAL ROLE.

WHEN A SWEAT LODGE WAS IN USE, ITS
FRAME WAS COVERED AND THE ROCKS INSIDE
WERE HEATED. WATER THROWN ON THE HOT ROCKS
BATHED THE YOUNG BOY IN PURIFYING STEAM.

After experiencing a vision, the boy would rejoin the tribe. The medicine man or another old and wise man would be waiting for him. He would help the boy to understand what he saw. The image or vision seen by the boy on his quest would now provide him with a protector from the spirit world.

Medicine men were important individuals within the tribe. It was believed that they had the ability to foresee the future as well as to heal. Both men and women acted as healers. Also, women were sought after as midwives.

The tribe's oldest and most honored holy men conducted a yearly summer ritual known as the Sun Dance. The Sun Dance was an important religious ceremony. It lasted for twelve days.

During the Sun Dance some participants engaged in painful self-mutilation as a tribute to the Grandfather Spirit. No one was forced to take part in the Sun Dance. Those who wanted to, volunteered. They demonstrated a great deal of personal courage and endurance for their beliefs.

THE SUN DANCE WAS A SACRED RELIGIOUS RITUAL
HELD EVERY YEAR IN THE SUMMER.

Another important part of the Sioux's religion was the Sacred Pipe. Used during prayer, it was believed to link the individual to the Great Mystery Power. Most Sioux men had their own pipes which they used during religious rituals. The tribe also owned a number of elaborately decorated pipes. These were reserved for the most sacred ceremonies.

DELICATELY CARVED CEREMONIAL PIPES WERE BELIEVED TO HAVE ESPECIALLY STRONG POWERS. THESE PIPES WERE ADORNED WITH PIECES OF FUR, HORSEHAIR BANDS, AND COLORFUL QUILLS. SOME HAD BEAUTIFULLY CARVED STEMS THAT EXTENDED FOUR OR FIVE FEET.

AND THEN THE WHITES CAME

The Sioux hunted the buffalo on the plains for more than a century. They were a proud, independent, and courageous people. However, their lives were dramatically changed forever with the coming of the whites.

By the 1840s white settlers had discovered that there was good black soil in some areas of the plains. They were determined to remain to farm the fertile land. In addition, gold had been found in California. Thousands responded to the call, *Go west, young man*. Hordes of people now trafficked across the Indians' grasslands.

As these would-be miners needed a food supply, they slaughtered thousands of buffalo along the way. To make things worse, there were now far less buffalo. Wagon trains heading west had trampled over the animals' breeding and feeding grounds, causing the herds to scatter. Life had already become difficult for

AT TIMES, WHITE SOLDIERS MARCHED ON SIOUX CAMPS AND OPENED FIRE WITHOUT WARNING. RIFLE BULLETS SAILED THROUGH THE AIR AND TORE OPEN THE BUFFALO SKIN TIPI COVERS.

the Indians, who had always depended on the buffalo for their survival.

At first the Indians did not strike the wagon trains heading west. Perhaps they believed that the whites' invasion was only temporary. But severe injustices and cruelties on the part of white soldiers and settlers eventually led to prolonged bloodshed between the Sioux and the whites.

THE INDIANS' STYLE OF WARFARE PUT THEM
AT A DISADVANTAGE WHEN FIGHTING WHITES.
THEIR OBJECT IN BATTLE WAS NOT SO MUCH TO
DESTROY THE ENEMY AS TO WIN PERSONAL HONOR.
ONE IMPORTANT INDIAN PRACTICE IN BATTLE
WAS COUNTING COUP. A WARRIOR SCORED A COUP
IF HE TOUCHED HIS ENEMY WITH A COUP STICK.

Warfare between the whites and the Sioux was brutal and enduring. The issues separating the two sides were clear. The whites wanted the Indians' land. They wanted land for farming, to graze their sheep and cattle, and to mine for precious metals. And they were determined to do whatever they had to in order to get it.

Most of the white settlers had little respect for the Indians, whose lands they were anxious to take over. To the whites, the Indians were savages who did not work the land to its fullest advantage. To the Indians, the encroaching white settlers became a destructive force that had to be dealt with if the Sioux were to survive as a people.

THE STRUGGLE CONTINUES

The Sioux could boast of a number of outstanding leaders among their people. One was a great chief named Red Cloud. Red Cloud had tried to reason with the white soldiers to close a passage known as the Bozeman Trail. The trail, which was heavily used by white settlers, ran directly through much of the buffalo country. But after the whites tried to trick Red Cloud, the talks broke off. Skirmishes along the route were so common that the path came to be called the Bloody Bozeman.

The fighting between the Indians and the whites peaked on December 21, 1866. A group of white soldiers working along the Bozeman Trail were ambushed by a band of Red Cloud's warriors. Actually, this tactic was just a hoax. Red Cloud had only staged the raid so that the cavalry would send out reinforcements to help their men.

The cavalry took the bait. Captain William J. Fetterman had often expressed anti-Indian feelings. Now the Bozeman incident gave him a chance to do as he wished. Fetterman, along with eighty soldiers, rode rapidly out of the fort to put down the Sioux attack. But this was exactly what Red Cloud had hoped for.

The Sioux chief wanted Fetterman to think that the cavalry was winning. So he had a number of his warriors retreat. Fetterman rode deeper into Sioux country. He went far past the border at which he had been ordered to stop. Fetterman soon found himself in the middle of the Indians' heaviest forces. There he and his soldiers lost their lives in the fighting that followed.

Even after his victory, Red Cloud and his men continued their struggle to force the government to close the path. Finally, in 1868, the government abandoned the Bozeman Trail. Triumphantly, Red Cloud rode through the deserted army fort along the Bozeman and burned it to the ground.

Nevertheless, Red Cloud's victory could not alter the Indians' fate. Gains made against the soldiers did not make up for the disappearing buffalo herds. In 1800, before large numbers of white settlers overtook Indian territory, more than sixty million buffalo roamed the plains. Within the next fifty years, that number drastically dropped.

WHITE GENTLEMEN TRAVELING WEST SHOT AT BUFFALOS
FROM THE WINDOWS OF THEIR LUXURIOUS, SLOW-MOVING
RAILROAD COACHES. IT WAS A CRUEL AND WASTEFUL
ACTIVITY, BUT THE SPORT BECAME QUITE POPULAR.

In the 1860s, when the whites began to build railways across the country, the massive destruction of the buffalo began. The railroad builders did not want to go to the bother and expense of importing meat from the East for their crews. Instead, they hired professional hunters to kill buffalo for them. In this way they were provided with a readily available food source for their workers. In addition, shooting buffalo became a great means of entertainment for sportsmen traveling west.

Things worsened for the buffalo in the 1870s. A Pennsylvania company realized that buffalo hides could be tanned and sold to customers as leather. Renewed groups of whites went west to try their luck at becoming professional buffalo hunters.

These individuals earned their living by killing buffalo. Skilled buffalo hunters could kill and skin as many as fifty buffalo a day. Meanwhile, the slain animals' meat was left to rot.

The massive slaughter of the American buffalo helped to destroy the Indians' way of life. Unfortunately, the destruction was encouraged by the white people's government. The Indians had depended on the buffalo for survival. They never killed for sport or pleasure and had not been wasteful in their use of the animal.

The loss of the buffalo had robbed the Indians living on the plains of a means to meet their most basic needs. A people who had once lived with abundance now faced starvation.

LITTLE BIGHORN

Many plains Indian tribes fell victim to both frequent attacks by white soldiers and the dwindling buffalo herds. They grew poor and desperate and were no longer able to live as their people had in the past. The government forced a number of tribes onto *reservations*. These were separate parcels of land on which the Indians lived in extreme poverty.

Yet in some places the Indians clung fiercely to what was theirs. They kept their religious beliefs and practiced their ancient rituals. They scoured the region to track the now scarce buffalo herds. The Sioux Indians were among these tribes.

The Sioux, along with several other tribes, had managed to keep one special area free of white settlers. This was the Black Hills of the Dakota country. Since the hills were sacred to the Sioux, the government had promised that the grounds would remain untouched.

However, in 1874, a lieutenant colonel named George Armstrong Custer commanded a special expedition into the Dakota Black Hills. Custer and his men reported that the Black Hills were rich with gold. As a result, hordes of prospectors swarmed the hills in search of the precious ore. The Indians' treaty rights to the area, which had been guaranteed by the government, were ignored.

The Indians tried to defend their sacred land that had been abused by the prospectors. Hundreds of Sioux raided white settlements while valiantly resisting the government's efforts to round them up.

It was at this time that Sitting Bull, one of the Sioux's most honored leaders, came to power. At first Sitting Bull had not been in favor of fighting the whites. He had hoped that the settlers and soldiers would leave just as they had come and that the Indians would be free to lead their lives as they wished.

But it soon became clear that the whites had no intention of leaving. Sitting Bull refused to submit to the whites' demands. Countless other Sioux followed his example.

Then, on June 25, 1876, one of the most famous showdowns between the U.S. Cavalry and the Indians occurred. Lt. Col. George Armstrong Custer was sent

A SYMBOLIC DEPICTION OF THE
PRINCIPAL PEOPLE INVOLVED AT THE
BATTLE OF LITTLE BIGHORN:
LT. COL. GEORGE ARMSTRONG CUSTER,
CRAZY HORSE, AND SITTING BULL.

to scout out the area near the east bank of the Little Bighorn River in Montana. He had been given orders to find rebellious Sioux and Cheyennes but had been warned not to take any action until reinforcements arrived.

Custer was a reckless and impatient man. He was anxious to do battle with the Indians so that he could claim a victory for himself. He decided to disobey orders and attack.

By midafternoon the battle between Custer and the Indians was underway. The Indians moved quickly, pinning the white cavalry soldiers against the hills. Sioux war chiefs such as Gall and Crazy Horse led hundreds of mounted warriors in swift and punishing charges against the white soldiers.

It was the largest number of Indians ever to do battle with a U.S. Cavalry unit. The Indians easily overtook the regiment's defenses. The battle at Little Bighorn proved to be the Indians' great military triumph.

HARD TIMES

The victory won by the Indians at Little Bighorn was short-lived. In the following weeks the U.S. government sent massive cavalry reinforcements into what had once been Indian territory. The soldiers carefully combed the area to hunt down the starving Indian bands still struggling to survive.

Conditions worsened greatly for the plains Indians. As time passed, it became futile for them to continue to resist the whites. In less than five years following the Little Bighorn victory, few tribespeople freely roamed the plains as they once had.

Then, in 1881, Sitting Bull and his band of exhausted and hungry followers were forced to surrender to the U.S. Army. The man who had fought so long for the Indians' way of life was confined to a reservation.

The glory that had once been the Sioux's and other plains tribes' had tarnished. The people were now made wards of the government and forced onto reservations. They were given barren land on which to grow crops. In addition, each year Congress continued to cut the amount of money set aside for the reservation Indians.

To worsen matters, governmental agencies pressured the Indians to sell off portions of their reservations to new white settlers. As a result, in the 1880s Sioux Indians on the Dakota reservations were near starvation.

During that bleak period the Sioux were encouraged by news from a reservation in faraway Nevada. There an Indian prophet had had a vision in which the white invaders had disappeared and the tribespeople who had been killed returned from the dead. The prophet had predicted a new age of good fortune for the Indian people.

Believers in the prophecy took part in a simple ceremony of chants and communal dancing called the Ghost Dance. Although the spirit of the Ghost Dance was antiwhite, its followers were forbidden to bear arms. Nevertheless, the army viewed the Ghost Dance as a threat. They feared that the Indians might rise up to fight them.

UNFORTUNATELY, THE WHITES TRIED TO FORCE
THEIR WAY OF LIFE ON THE SIOUX. THESE ARE
SIOUX BOYS AS THEY WERE DRESSED ON THEIR
ARRIVAL AT THE CARLISLE INDIAN SCHOOL.

THE GHOST DANCE. A GROUP OF SIOUX FROM THE
DAKOTA RESERVATIONS JOURNEYED TO NEVADA
TO HEAR ABOUT THE GHOST DANCE FROM THE
PROPHET HIMSELF. WORD OF THE GHOST DANCE
QUICKLY SPREAD THROUGHOUT THE GRASSLANDS.

In 1890 troops were sent to the Pine Ridge Reservation to stop the Ghost Dance. The government also decided to arrest Sitting Bull, who had been staying at a nearby reservation known as the Standing Rock Reservation. Government officials thought that he might be encouraging the Ghost Dance among the Sioux.

On December 15, 1890, forty-three police arrived to arrest the Sioux leader. As Sitting Bull was being taken out of his cabin, he managed to break free from his captors. Fighting broke out, and the police fired into the crowd. By the time the scuffle had finished, fourteen people were dead. Sitting Bull was among those killed.

Even in defeat Sitting Bull had been greatly respected as a leader by his people. With his death, panic overtook the reservation. Large numbers of Sioux ran from the area. The government sent troops to round them up and return them to their former confines.

WOUNDED KNEE

With Sitting Bull's death nearly four hundred of his followers had fled the reservation. They feared the white government's reaction to their involvement in the Ghost Dance. The runaways had hoped to seek shelter with other Sioux under Chief Big Foot at the Cheyenne River Reservation.

Many Sioux were rounded up by white soldiers along the way. Only a handful finished the journey to Big Foot's village, but the situation had grown tense there as well. The cavalry had gotten word of where the runaways were heading. Soon the reservation was surrounded by white soldiers.

Big Foot and his people feared that they might be killed during a confrontation with the soldiers. So during the night of December 28, 1890, the chief, along with about 350 of his followers, silently crept out of the camp. They were soon pursued by armed soldiers on horseback.

FOLLOWING THE MASSACRE AT WOUNDED KNEE,
WHITE CIVILIANS WERE PAID $2.00 FOR
EACH INDIAN BODY THEY PLOWED INTO THE
COMMON GRAVE IN THE FROZEN EARTH.

IN 1903 SIOUX INDIANS ERECTED A MONUMENT
OVER THE MASS GRAVE AT WOUNDED KNEE.

On December 29th a group of the Indians surrendered to the cavalrymen. Before taking them back to the reservation, the soldiers had the Indians camp for the night at a spot called Wounded Knee. The next morning the soldiers required the Indians to turn in their weapons.

When the Indians refused to obey, the soldiers used force. Fighting broke out, and within minutes a shot was heard. At that point the white soldiers seemed to go crazy. They fired their rifles wildly into the crowd. The soldiers even killed a number of their own men accidentally.

The Indians tried to resist the soldiers' attack. But the soldiers shot everyone in sight. Even mothers trying to escape with their young were ruthlessly gunned down. The peaceful campsite had been turned into a bloody slaughter scene.

Close to three hundred Sioux were killed. Twenty-five soldiers died too. The white cavalrymen were buried with full military honors. Several days after the massacre, a crew was hired to plow the Indians' bodies into a large pit that served as a common grave.

Wounded Knee ended the Sioux Indians' armed struggle against the whites. However, the massacre that took place there remains a symbol of the brutality and injustice endured by a once-free people.

TODAY

Over the past century, life for the Sioux as well as for other Indian tribes has not been easy. Modern Indians have had to face many of the same problems their ancestors had known since the whites arrived.

Today some Indians have chosen to leave the reservations, while others have remained. Although some Indians have become successful professionals, many still live in poverty. In addition, large numbers of Indians have been victims of fatal childhood diseases due to poor diet and medical care. They have lived with high unemployment rates and poor housing conditions. Alcoholism has been a problem on many reservations.

In spite of their hardships, though, American Indians have survived. Within their communities, many Sioux have tried to maintain their traditional tribal values. They have stressed family loyalties, tribal ties, and their own religious views to their children.

FEW EMPLOYMENT OPPORTUNITIES AND
POOR HOUSING HAVE MADE LIFE DIFFICULT
ON MANY SIOUX RESERVATIONS.

PRESERVING THEIR ANCIENT TRIBAL CUSTOMS AND
DANCES, HERE THE SIOUX YELLOW HAND DANCE TROUPE
PERFORMS AT FT. ROBEINSON STATE PARK, NEBRASKA.
FACING PAGE: BEAUTIFULLY DESIGNED, COLORFUL
BEADWORK (AS WORN BY THIS SIOUX WOMAN)
REMAINS HIGHLY PRIZED TODAY.

In recent years numerous Indian groups have called attention to their problems and demanded justice. In 1944 the National Congress of American Indians (NCAI) was formed to promote helpful legislation. On a regional level, local groups, such as the United Sioux Tribes, have dealt with problems in specific locations.

These groups are convinced that American Indians share a proud and valuable heritage. Their past and culture are worthy of respect. They are the first Americans.

FOR FURTHER READING

Behrens, June. *Powwow*. Chicago: Children's Press, 1983.

Ewers, John C. *Blackfeet Crafts*. Stevens Point, Wisconsin: Schneider Publications, 1986.

Glubok, Shirley. *The Art of the Plains Indians*. New York: Macmillan, 1975.

Green, Carl R. and Sanford, William R. *The Bison*. Mankato, Minnesota: Crestwood House Inc., 1985.

Martini, Teri. *Indians*. Chicago: Children's Press, 1982.

Smith, Kathie. *Sitting Bull*. New York: Julian Messner, 1987.

Stein, R. C. *The Story of Wounded Knee*. Chicago: Children's Press, 1983.

Troughton, Joanna. *How Rabbit Stole the Fire: A North American Indian Folk Tale*. New York: P. Bendrick Books, 1986.

Wheeler, M. J. *First Came the Indians*. New York: Macmillan, 1983.

INDEX

ABOUT THE AUTHOR

*Elaine Landau has been
a newspaper reporter, a
youth services librarian, and
a children's book editor.*

*She has written over twenty
books for young people.*

*Ms. Landau makes her home
in Sparta, New Jersey.*

BLc1

j978　　Landau, Elaine.
LAN
　　　　The Sioux

$11.90

1/2/91